TAPAS

Colophon

© 2002 Rebo International b.v., Lisse, The Netherlands

www.rebo-publishers.com - info@rebo-publishers.com

Original recipes and photographs: © R&R Publishing Pty. Ltd.

Design and layout: Minkowsky Graphics, Enkhuizen, The Netherlands

Typesetting: AdAm Studio, Prague, The Czech Republic

Cover design: Minkowsky Graphics, Enkhuizen, The Netherlands

Proofreading: Jarmila Pešková Škraňáková, Joshua H. Joseph

ISBN 90 366 1601 8

TAPAS

sun-drenched delights for
creative cooking

REBO
PUBLISHERS

Foreword

Tapas are delicious starters, snacks, or appetizers served with drinks in Spanish cafes and bars. The Spanish word tapa (meaning to cover) points to the earlier function of tapas: a piece of ham or bread was used to cover a glass of sherry against flies and mosquitoes.

This book is full of ideas to help you make a wide variety of tapas— sweet or savory; simple or exquisite. From *Spicy Olives* and *Stuffed Grape Leaves* to *Carpaccio of Beef* and *Watermelon with Lemon Syrup*—these recipes are sure to tantalize your tastebuds.

Serve the tapas hot or cold, in small earthenware dishes and enjoy with a glass of ice-cold sangria or dry sherry—a guaranteed fiesta!

Abbreviations

All measurements conform to European and American measurement systems. For easier cooking, the American cup measurement is used throughout the book.

tbsp = tablespoon
tsp = teaspoon
oz = ounce
lb = pound
°F = degrees Fahrenheit
°C = degrees Celsius

g = gram
kg = kilogram
cm = centimeter
ml = mililiter
l = liter
qt = quart

Method

Cut off the hard base of the asparagus.

Cook the asparagus for 4 minutes in boiling water until they become tender, but still crisp.

Rinse with cold water and pat dry with paper towels. Pour the lemon juice in a bowl for the dressing.

Add the oil slowly and allow the mixture to thicken while stirring. Season the dressing with salt and pepper.

Pour the dressing over the asparagus and serve with pecorino shavings and the pieces of pancetta.

Ingredients

1lb 2oz/500g fresh asparagus

juice of 1 lemon

½ cup olive oil, extra virgin

pecorino cheese shavings

8 thin slices of pancetta, in pieces

freshly ground pepper

sea salt

Asparagus with Pecorino
and Pancetta

Method

Preheat oven to 400°F/200°C. Slice all potatoes in half and mix them with the oil in a bowl. Season with salt and pepper and place them on a greased baking sheet with the sliced end facing down. Bake for about 20 minutes until they become soft. Leave potatoes to cool.

Mix, in the meantime, the finely cut salmon, sour cream, onions, horseradish, and chives in a small bowl and add salt and pepper. Create a small hollow in the potato halves and slice the top of the round ends so that they can stand upright.

Stuff the potatoes with a teaspoon of the salmon stuffing and place on a serving dish.

Garnish each potato with a small square of salmon, some salmon caviar, and finely chopped chives.

Place them in the fridge to chill for about 2 hours before serving.

New Potatoes with Smoked Salmon

Ingredients

24 new potatoes

5oz/150g smoked salmon, finely cut

2 tbsp Bermuda onions, finely chopped

a small bag of fresh chives, finely chopped

2oz/50g thinly sliced smoked salmon, in 24 small squares

extra chive sprigs for garnishing

1 tbsp olive oil

salt and pepper

3 tbsp sour cream

1 tsp white horseradish

salmon caviar

capers

Method

Put the mustard in a bowl, add vinegar, sugar, salt, pepper, and herbs. Mix well.

Add olive oil while stirring. Cover the bowl and set aside the vinaigrette until needed. Steam the asparagus for 5 to 10 minutes until just tender, but ensure that they are still crisp.

Place the asparagus on a plate and sprinkle them with the vinaigrette.

Serve hot or cold.

Asparagus in Vinaigrette

Ingredients

1 tbsp Dijon mustard

4 tbsp red wine vinegar

$\frac{1}{2}$ tsp sugar; $\frac{1}{4}$ tsp salt

$\frac{1}{4}$ tsp freshly ground black pepper

fresh parsley, finely chopped

fresh chives, finely chopped

$\frac{1}{2}$ cup olive oil; 1 bundle of asparagus

Method

Cut the eggplants in half (leave the stalks). Lightly coat the cut sides with canola oil.

Heat a nonstick frying pan over medium heat.

Place the eggplants in the pan with the round sides facing upwards and fry gently until golden brown. Take the eggplants from the pan.

Cook the garlic, ginger, cumin seeds, chili powder, and 1 tablespoon of water in the same pan. Cook this mixture until the garlic is tender, then turn the heat to low.

Stir in soy sauce, lemon juice, and $\frac{1}{2}$ cup of water and leave the sauce to simmer for a few minutes. Place the eggplants back in the pan and cook for about 10 minutes until they are tender and have absorbed most of the sauce.

Add basil and serve on a dish.

Ingredients

8 thin eggplants

3 cloves of garlic, crushed

1 tbsp fresh ginger, grated

$\frac{1}{2}$ tsp cumin seeds

a pinch of chili powder

1 tbsp sweet soy sauce

2 tbsp lemon juice

about 10 leaves of Asian basil

canola oil

Eggplant with Ginger and Soy Sauce

Method

Heat the oil in a frying pan and fry the flaked almonds until golden brown. Remove them from the pan with a skimmer and drain on paper towel.

Add the onions and fry until tender. Add salt and herbs and fry everything another 2-3 minutes. Add the pieces of chicken and fry while stirring until done.

Add tomatoes, raisins, parsley, flaked almonds, and wine, then simmer completely covered for 15 minutes. Take the lid off the pan and cook until all the juices have been absorbed. Allow to cool. Thaw out the filo pastry according to the instructions on the packet.

Remove 14 sheets and put the rest back in the freezer. Place the sheets with the long side parallel to the worktop. Cut each sheet into three strips of 6 in/15cm. Lay the strips on top of one another and cover with a clean dish towel. Take 2 strips for each piece, lightly cover with canola oil and fold in half lengthwise.

Preheat the oven to 350°F/180°C. Place a teaspoon of the stuffing on the bottom of the strips of pastry. Fold the lower right corner of both strips to the corresponding upper left corner, making a triangle. Fold the lower left corner to the lower right corner.

Repeat with the other strips of pastry. Coat the upper side with plenty of canola oil. Place the triangles on an oil–coated baking sheet. Coat the upper side of the triangles with oil and bake for 20 to 25 minutes in the oven. Serve hot.

Chicken Almond Triangles

Ingredients

1 tbsp olive oil

2¹/₂ oz/60g flaked almonds

1 onion finely chopped

¹/₄ tsp salt; ¹/₂ tsp cinnamon powder

1 tbsp paprika; 1 tsp cumin powder

1lb 2oz/500g chicken slices

2 small tomatoes, chopped

2oz/55g chopped raisins

2 tbsp fresh parsley, finely chopped

¹/₄ cup dry white wine

1 packet of frozen filo pastry, canola oil

Variation for the stuffing

9 oz/255g stir-fried pieces of chicken and 1 finely chopped onion

mixed with 9 oz/255g ricotta and 1 beaten egg.

Method

Preheat oven to 425°F/220°C. Halve the lemon, squeeze one half, and chop the other into small pieces.

Halve the large new potatoes. Mix the potatoes, lemon juice, pieces of lemon, garlic, and oil. Season with salt and pepper and spoon the mixture into a shallow baking pan. Place pats of butter over the mixture.

Bake for 25 to 30 minutes—shake the baking pan regularly—until the potatoes are tender and golden brown. Add the pieces of olive shortly before serving.

New Potatoes with Lemon and Olives

Ingredients

1 lemon

1lb 10oz/750g fresh new potatoes

2 cloves garlic

2 tbsp olive oil

salt and black pepper

1 tbsp butter

2oz/60g green olives pitted, quartered

tapas

Method

Mix the olive oil, lemon rind and juice, shallots, oregano, salt, and pepper in a large bowl.

Add the squid and marinate for about 1 hour.

Heat a boiling pan (or set the broiler to the highest temperature) and coat with oil. Add the squid, sprinkle with marinade, and broil for about 2 to 3 minutes until tender.

Serve the squid on a bed of arugula.

Ingredients

¹/₂ cup olive oil

rind of 1 lemon

2 tbsp lemon juice

2oz/50g shallots, chopped

1 tsp oregano, finely chopped

freshly ground pepper and salt

1lb 10oz/750 g small squid, ready to cook

arugula salad for garnishing

Squid in Olive Oil and Oregano

Method

Brush a sheet of waxed baking paper with oil and sprinkle with salt and pepper.

Place four slices of beef, approximately 2in/5cm from one another. Place on top of this another sheet of oiled baking paper and beat until the beef has doubled in size. Put the meat in the fridge until ready for use.

Place some arugula in the middle of a plate and arrange the slices of beef around it. Sprinkle with balsamic vinegar, olive oil, pecorino, and pepper.

Beef Carpaccio

Ingredients

1 tbsp oil

1lb/450g beef fillet in slices ¼ in/½ cm thick

4oz/125g arugula, washed

1 tbsp balsamic vinegar

¼ cup extra virgin olive oil

pecorino shavings

salt and freshly ground black pepper

Method

Scrub the mussels well and remove any beard. Put them in a large pan with the shallots, bay leaf, and sprigs of thyme and parsley.

Add salt and pour in the wine.

Steam the mussels for about 5 minutes until they open. Remove the upper shell of each mussel and discard.

Distribute the mussels in the shell evenly over ovenproof plates. Prepare herb butter using the butter, finely chopped parsley, garlic, and finely chopped chives. Cover each mussel generously with this mixture.

Cook the mussels for about 3 minutes at 375°F/190°C or until the herb butter has melted.

Ingredients

30 mussels

2 shallots, finely chopped

4oz/125g soft butter or margarine

1 tbsp fresh parsley, finely chopped

2 cloves garlic, crushed

2 sprigs of parsley

¼ cup white wine

1 tbsp fresh chives, finely chopped

1 bay leaf

1 sprig of thyme

¼ tsp salt

Mussels with Herbs

Method

Preheat the oven to 375°F/190°C. Cut the underside of the onions with a sharp knife so that they stand upright. Chop off the top of the onions and make two deep grooves in the middle. Place 2 half sprigs of rosemary and 2 strips of garlic in each onion and place the onions in a small roasting pan.

Mix the olive oil, balsamic vinegar, sugar, red wine vinegar, and vegetable stock in a small bowl.

Pour this sauce over the onions and roast for about 1½ hours until tender (check this by pricking the onion with a sharp knife). Pour the sauce over the onions regularly. Cut off the skin of each onion before serving and discard (or allow guests the pleasure).

Season with salt and pepper.

Roasted Onions with Balsamic Vinegar

Ingredients

8 red onions, in skin

8 sprigs rosemary

6 garlic cloves (peeled and in very thin strips)

¼ cup olive oil

1 tbsp brown sugar

⅔ cup vegetable stock

salt and freshly ground black pepper

2 tbsp balsamic vinegar

2 tbsp red wine vinegar

Method

Preheat the oven to 400°F/200°C.

Put the ricotta, feta, and eggs in a bowl and mix well. Season with white pepper.

Thaw out the filo pastry according to the instructions on the packet. Brush a sheet of filo pastry with some melted butter and place another sheet on top. Cut the pastry in four strips lengthwise.

Put a heaping teaspoon of the cheese-egg mixture onto the lower end of the pastry strip. Fold the lower right corner to the upper left corner, thereby making a triangle. Fold the lower left corner to the lower right corner. Fold the pastry as many times as possible and repeat for the other strips.

Brush the upper side of the triangle with the melted butter and place on a baking sheet. Bake them in the oven for 20 minutes until golden brown.

Ingredients

11oz/310g ricotta

11oz/310g feta

4 eggs

white pepper

1 packet of frozen filo pastry

4oz/125g melted butter

Cheese Triangles

Variation

For larger triangles, cut the pastry sheet into wider

strips and use more stuffing per triangle.

Method

Broil the slices of ciabatta 2-3 minutes per side.

Sprinkle generously with olive oil and brush with tomato puree. Finish off the ciabatta with slices of mozzarella and some basil.

Ciabatta with Mozzarella and Basil

Ingredients

1 ciabatta, in two 1in/2½ cm thick slices

⅓ cup sun-dried tomato puree

6oz/180g mozzarella balls, each ball cut into 5 slices

4oz/100g basil leaves, finely chopped or whole

4 tbsp olive oil

Method

Mix the chicken, shallots, bouquet garni, honey, lemon balm, and breadcrumbs in a food processor.

Roll the mixture into balls with wet hands. Place them on a flat plate and put in the fridge for 30 minutes.

Heat a layer of oil 2in/5cm deep to 350°F/180°C. Fry the balls for 3 to 4 minutes and then drain on paper towel.

Put a cocktail stick into each ball and place them on a plate.

Put all the ingredients for the plum sauce in a small pan and bring to a boil while stirring.

Simmer the sauce for 2 minutes.

Take the sauce off the heat and allow to cool.

Pour the sauce into a jug and serve with the chicken balls.

Ingredients

1lb 2oz/500g minced chicken

10 shallots, finely chopped

pinch of bouquet garni

1½ tbsp honey

½ tsp lemon balm

⅓ cup fresh breadcrumbs

oil for frying

For the plum sauce

11oz/300g plum jam

½ cup organic vinegar

pinch of spicy chili powder

⅛ tsp ginger

⅛ tsp allspice

Chicken Balls in Plum Sauce

Method

Scrub the mussels well and remove beard. Dispose of any open or damaged mussels. Put the mussels in a large pan with the wine and garlic. Place a lid on the pan and cook for 3 minutes over high heat until they open. Shake the pan regularly. Throw the still-closed mussels away.

Remove the upper shell of each mussel.

Mix all the ingredients for the garlic butter in a bowl. Place the mixture in the shells and broil until the mussels start to sizzle.

Serve with freshly baked baguette.

Mussel Escargot

Ingredients

2¼ lbs/1kg mussels

½ cup dry white wine

2 cloves garlic, crushed

For the garlic butter

1lb 2oz/500g soft butter

2 cloves garlic, chopped

1 tbsp fresh parsley, chopped

2 tbsp cognac; salt and pepper

Method

Beat the eggs in a bowl and season with salt and pepper.

Remove the donax clams from their shells and add them to the egg mixture.

Mix the breadcrumbs with the mixed herbs.

Roll the clams over the breadcrumb mixture. Shake them to remove any excess breadcrumbs. Deep-fry the shellfish in oil at 360°F/185°C for a few minutes until golden brown. Drain on paper towel and serve immediately with tartar sauce and slices of lemon.

Deep-fried Donax Clams

Ingredients

2 eggs

2¼ lbs/1kg donax clams, in the shell

½ cup breadcrumbs

1 tbsp mixed dried herbs

salt and pepper

oil for deep-frying

3 tbsp tartar sauce

lemon slices

Method

Preheat the oven to 350°F/180°C. Make triangles of the chicken wings and place them in a large roasting pan. Mix the remaining ingredients, apart from the sesame seeds, in a bowl and pour over the chicken.

Roast the chicken wings for 25 to 30 minutes until brown and done. Turn them over a few times during roasting. Take the chicken wings out of the oven and place them on a plate. Sprinkle with sesame seeds and serve immediately.

Chicken Wings with Fresh Ginger

Ingredients

2¹/₄ lbs/1kg chicken wings

2 garlic cloves, crushed

¹/₂ tsp soy sauce

4 tbsp fresh ginger, grated

3 tbsp sherry

2 tbsp sesame seeds

2 tbsp oil

2 tbsp sugar

Method

Sift the flour into a bowl. Add the butter and salt and knead until the mixture begins to resemble breadcrumbs. Mix the egg with the sour cream, then add this to the flour mixture and knead to create a dough.

Cover in plastic foil and place in the fridge for 30 minutes.

Heat the butter in a pan, add the onions, and fry for 2 to 3 minutes.

Add the pieces of chicken and fry while stirring until golden brown.

Stir in the pieces of peach and the salt and pepper. Allow the mixture to cool.

Roll the dough out between two sheets of waxed paper. Remove the upper sheet, and cut circles of 4x8in/10x20cm diameter out of the dough.

Preheat the oven to 400°F/200°C. Spoon 1 heaping teaspoon of stuffing into the middle of each dough circle. Moisten the edges with a little water, fold the dough in half and press the edges well with a fork.

Brush these semicircles with milk and bake for about 10 to 15 minutes in the oven.

Serve the empanadillas cold or hot, as a snack, or served as a meal with vegetables.

Ingredients

For the pasty dough

1lb/450g/3¾ cups flour

1 egg

1 tbsp milk

6oz/180g butter

a pinch of salt

¾ cup sour cream

For the stuffing

1½ tbsp butter or oil

1lb/2oz/500g chicken slices

4oz/100g canned peaches, finely chopped

salt and pepper

1 onion, chopped

Chicken Empanadillas

Method

Preheat the oven to 350 °F/180°C.

Mix the almonds, macadamia nuts, cashew nuts, and peanuts in a bowl.

Add the bouquet garni and the chili powder. Stir well.

Mix the soy sauce with the sesame oil and pour over the nuts until all are covered.

Scatter the nuts over a nonstick baking sheet and roast for about 15 minutes until they dry out and the soy sauce layer darkens.

Allow to cool. You can keep the nuts for approximately one month in an airtight container.

Ingredients

4oz/100g almonds with skin

4oz/100g macadamia nuts

4oz/100g unsalted cashew nuts

4oz/100g unsalted peanuts with skin

$\frac{1}{2}$ tsp bouquet garni

$\frac{1}{8}$ tsp chili powder

3 tbsp mild soy sauce

$\frac{1}{2}$ tsp sesame oil

Roasted Nuts with Chili and Soy sauce

Method

Scrub the mussels well. Immerse in cold water for 5 minutes, then allow to drain. Repeat. Remove beard and discard any damaged or opened mussels. Place the mussels in a large pan with the wine and garlic. Put a lid on the pan and cook for 3 minutes over high heat until they open. Shake the pan regularly. Throw the still-closed mussels away.

Take the mussels out of the pan and reserve the stock. Remove the upper half of each mussel and place the mussels on a baking sheet. Sieve the leftover stock in the pan through a clean dish towel. Put the ham, breadcrumbs, pesto, and ginger in a bowl, add 1 to 2 tablespoons of the stock and stir well.

Set the broiler to the highest temperature.

Cover each mussel with a layer of the mixture and broil the mussels for 2 minutes until golden brown.

Mussels with Ginger and Pesto

Ingredients

4¹⁄₂ lb/2kg fresh mussels

¹⁄₂ cup dry white wine

2 cloves garlic, crushed

4 slices of Parma ham, finely cut

¹⁄₂ cup fresh white breadcrumbs

1 tsp pesto

1 tsp fresh ginger, grated

Method

Put the oil, onion, red bell pepper, tomato, celery, and garlic in
a large pan and fry over high heat for about 5 minutes. Stir regularly
to keep ingredients from sticking to the pan.

Add the oysters, wine, and herbs, then season with salt and pepper.
Put the lid on the pan and cook the oysters until they open. Stir
regularly to ensure that all oysters are done.

Serve the oysters with their shell in large bowls, together with
a salad or freshly baked baguette. Serve the oysters with a rosé or
white wine from Provence.

Ingredients

$\frac{1}{2}$ cup olive oil, extra virgin

1 onion, finely chopped

1 red bell pepper, in pieces

4 tomatoes ripened in wine

$\frac{1}{2}$ stick of celery, chopped

2 cloves garlic

$2\frac{1}{4}$ lb/1kg ready-to-cook oysters

$\frac{2}{3}$ cup dry white wine

1 tbsp finely chopped fresh herbs

(thyme, rosemary or marjoram)

salt and pepper

Oysters Provençale

Method

Preheat oven to 400°F/200°C. Cut off the mushroom stalks and chop finely along with two of the mushroom caps. Fry this mixture together with the scallions in the butter until soft. Take the pan off the heat and add tomato and breadcrumbs, then season according to taste with salt and pepper. Add half the grated cheese and mix well to complete the stuffing.

Brush the inside of the mushroom caps with pesto and carefully fill each cap with the stuffing. Place the caps on a waxed baking sheet and scatter the remaining grated cheese on top. Bake the caps just before serving for about 10 minutes in the oven (or until they are sufficiently hot and firm). Serve on small plates with small forks.

For the pesto: put the basil, garlic, pistachio nuts, and Parmesan cheese into the food processor and mix until the mixture is finely chopped. Add the oil until the pesto acquires the desired thickness. Season with salt and pepper. You can prepare the stuffed mushroom caps 8 hours in advance, and then bake them in the oven just before serving.

Mushroom Caps with Pesto Stuffing

Ingredients

14 mushrooms of similar size

4 scallions, finely chopped

1 tbsp unsalted butter

8 sun-dried tomatoes in oil, drained and finely chopped

1 tbsp dry breadcrumbs

3 tbsp Parmesan cheese (grated)

4 tbsp pesto (ready-made or home-made)

salt and pepper

For pesto

4-5oz/115-150g fresh basil leaves

2 cloves garlic, peeled

2oz/150g pistachio nuts, roasted

3 tbsp Parmesan cheese

$^2/_3$ cup olive oil

salt and pepper

Method

Mix the crab meat with the butter, mustard, Tabasco, egg yolk, and breadcrumbs in a bowl. Add salt according to taste. Cover the bowl and allow the mixture to become firm in the fridge.

Make balls from the crab mixture (about the size of a walnut) and place them in the fridge for another 30 minutes. Roll the balls in the flour and fry them in hot oil until golden brown. Drain the balls on paper towels and serve with tartar sauce.

Put all the ingredients for the tartar sauce in a bowl and mix well. Season with salt and pepper.

Cover the bowl and put the sauce in the fridge until required.

Ingredients

1lb 2oz/500g crab meat

2 tbsp soft butter

1 tbsp Dijon mustard

a few drops Tabasco sauce

2 egg yolks

2 tbsp fresh breadcrumbs

2 tbsp flour

oil for deep-frying

salt

For the tartar sauce

2 cups mayonnaise

$\frac{1}{2}$ tsp onion, finely chopped

$\frac{1}{2}$ tsp parsley, finely chopped

$\frac{1}{2}$ tsp basil, finely chopped

$\frac{1}{2}$ tsp gherkin, finely chopped

$\frac{1}{2}$ tsp green olives, finely chopped

$\frac{1}{2}$ tsp Dijon mustard

salt and freshly ground black pepper

Deep-fried Crab Balls

Method

Remove the oysters from their shells and place in the fridge. Wash the shells and arrange them on four ovenproof plates on a layer of sea salt. Heat the butter in a pan and fry the leek while stirring. Season with salt, pepper, and sugar.

Cover the pan well and leave to simmer. Sprinkle with lemon juice.

Bring the wine with the saffron and curry powder to a boil and boil until reduced to half.

Mix the cream with the egg yolk in a bowl and add this to the wine mixture. Stir continuously until the sauce thickens somewhat (do not allow to boil). Add salt and pepper and remove the pan from the heat.

Spoon some finely chopped leek into each shell and place the oysters on top.

Pour the sauce over the oysters and place them under a preheated broiler for several minutes. Serve immediately.

Spicy Oysters with Leek

Ingredients

20-24 large oysters with shell

granulated sea salt; 2 tbsp butter

freshly-squeezed lemon juice

1 thin leek, finely chopped

salt, freshly ground pepper

½ cup dry white wine

a few saffron threads or a pinch of curry powder

5oz/150g/1 cup creme fraiche

1 egg yolk

sugar

Method

Preheat oven to 490°F/250°C. Prepare the pizza dough as instructed on the packet. Sprinkle the baking sheet and kitchen worktop with some flour. Take a piece of pizza dough and roll with a rolling pin until a thick circle is formed.

Roll the circle in one direction, rotate, and then roll out in another direction. Repeat until the dough circle has a diameter of 3½in/8 cm. Continue with the rest of the dough (8 bases total).

Place the pizza bases on the baking sheet and brush them with chili oil. Cover the bases with slices of potato, onion, and rosemary, then bake the mini pizzas for 5 to 10 minutes until brown. Before serving, place some finely chopped arugula on top of the pizzas and sprinkle with some chili oil.

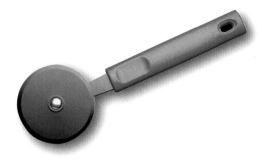

Mini Pizzas with Potato and Chili Oil

Ingredients

1 tbsp flour

1 packet of ready-made pizza dough

3 tbsp chili oil

4 potatoes, in thin slices

2 small red onions, finely sliced

3 sprigs of rosemary, finely chopped

a few arugula leaves for garnishing

Variation for garnishing

arugula and Parmesan cheese,

sun-dried tomatoes,

mozzarella balls and basil

Method

Mix the onion, rice, oil, herbs, salt, and two-thirds of the lemon juice in a bowl. Bring a pan of water to a boil and leave the grape leaves to soak for about 15 minutes.

Rinse the grape leaves with cold water and allow to dry on a clean dish towel.

Put one tablespoon of the rice stuffing in the middle of each leaf (for smaller leaves use less stuffing). Fold the sides of the leaves inward and roll firmly (starting with the stalk).

Place the dolmades in a pan and add boiling water until they are covered. Sprinkle with the remaining lemon juice. Place a reversed plate over the rolls and simmer for about 1 hour.

Ingredients

9oz/250g onion, finely chopped

14oz/400g short-grained rice, cooked

1 tbsp fresh dill, finely chopped

1 tbsp fresh mint, finely chopped

40 small grape leaves

$\frac{1}{2}$ cup lemon juice

$\frac{1}{2}$ tsp salt

$\frac{2}{3}$ cup oil

Stuffed Grape Leaves (Dolmades)

Method

Wash and pat dry the potatoes. Cut them into thin slices. Beat the eggs in a bowl. Heat the oil in a frying pan and add the potatoes and onion. Season with salt and cover the pan. Fry the potatoes gently. Shake the pan regularly to avoid sticking.

Remove potatoes when they are cooked, but not crispy and add to the beaten eggs. Mix everything well so that the potatoes are completely covered in egg. Add salt. Heat approximately 1 tablespoon of the remaining oil.

Put the egg and potato mixture back into the pan and fry for a few minutes until one side is golden brown. Prepare a plate that is a little larger than the pan. Let the omelet slide carefully onto the plate with the golden brown side facing down.

Slide back into the pan with the golden brown side facing up. Fry the omelet until it is firm; it should be about 2in/5cm thick. Cut into 1½in/4cm squares and serve as tapas.

Potato Omelet

Ingredients

2¼ lbs/1kg potatoes, peeled

1⅓ cup olive oil

5 eggs, beaten

1 small onion, peeled and roughly chopped (to taste)

salt

Method

Heat the oil in a pan and fry the garlic for 2 minutes over moderate heat.

Add the parsley, bay leaf, chili pepper, and shrimp, then fry for 2 minutes over moderate heat.

Pour the wine into the mixture and cook for a further 3 minutes until the shrimp is done and the wine has been reduced to half. Add salt and pepper according to taste.

Shrimp with Garlic and Wine Sauce

Ingredients

½ cup olive oil

6 cloves garlic, crushed

1 bunch of parsley, finely chopped

1 bay leaf

1 red chili pepper, finely chopped

2¼ lbs/1kg fresh shrimp, peeled

½ cup dry white wine

salt and pepper according to taste

Method

Preheat oven to 350°F/180°C. Grease eight large 10fl oz/300ml muffin forms with some canola oil.

Heat the oil in a frying pan and fry the mushrooms, scallions, and garlic for about 3 minutes over high heat. Allow the mixture to cool somewhat.

Put the mushroom mixture in a bowl, add Cheddar cheese, ricotta cheese, eggs, and nutmeg, then season with salt and pepper.

Cut the slices of ham into small strips and add to the mushroom mixture.

Place the slices of filo pastry on top of one another, and cut them in half lengthwise.

Cut each piece into 4 further pieces of equal size. Brush the four pieces of pastry with some canola oil and lay them in a muffin form; repeat for the rest. Spoon the stuffing into the forms with pastry.

Bake the tarts for 20 to 25 minutes in the oven until golden brown. Allow to cool for a few minutes, then remove from the forms. Serve the tarts with crispy green salad.

Ingredients

1 tbsp canola oil

4 oz/100g mushrooms, sliced

6 scallions, finely chopped

1 clove garlic, crushed

2 oz/50g Cheddar, grated

7 oz/200g ricotta cheese

1/4 tsp nutmeg; black pepper

6 slices (4oz/125g) of ham

4 sheets of filo pastry

1 tbsp olive oil

2 eggs

Ham and Mushrooms Tarts

tapas

Method

Put all the marinade ingredients in a bowl and mix well. Add the spare ribs, making sure they are well-covered by the mixture and leave to marinate for 4 hours in the fridge.

Remove the spare ribs from the marinade and allow to drain. Set aside the marinade. Broil the spare ribs on a preheated broiler for 6 to 8 minutes until tender and golden brown. Pour marinade over them regularly. Place them on a serving dish. Cover the dish and keep the spare ribs warm.

Pour the rest of the marinade into a small pan, add onions, parsley, stock, and lemon juice, and bring this mixture to a boil. Simmer the sauce over low heat for about 15 minutes until it has reduced by about half. Pour the sauce in the food processor and mix well, during which time you should add the melted butter.

Serve the sauce with the spare ribs.

Ingredients

4¹/₂ lb/2kg spare ribs (pork)

2 onions, finely chopped

2 tbsp fresh parsley, finely chopped

1¹/₃ cup chicken stock

2 tbsp lemon juice

4oz/125g melted butter

For the marinade

2 small red chili peppers, finely chopped

4 cloves garlic, crushed

2 scallions, finely chopped

¹/₂ tsp fresh ginger, grated

1³/₄ cup rice vinegar

¹/₂ cup mild soy sauce

6oz/170g honey

Spare Ribs with Honey and Soy Sauce

Method

Preheat oven to 425°F/215°C. Cut 4 circles 5 in/12cm in diameter from the puff pastry. Make a ¹⁄₂in/2cm edge on the circles using a sharp knife.

Place the pastry circles on a baking sheet. Heat the oil in a large frying pan and fry the onion for about 10 minutes until soft. Add the chili pepper and fry for another minute. Season the onion mixture with salt and pepper.

Brush the entire surface of the pastry circles with the pesto, except for the edges. Spoon the onion stuffing onto the pesto layer and scatter the pine nuts evenly over the circles. Bake the tarts for 12 to 15 minutes until they have risen and are golden brown.

Red Onion and Chili Pepper Tarts

Ingredients

13 oz/375g rolled out puff pastry

1 tbsp olive oil

7 oz/200g red onions, halved and chopped lengthwise

1 small red chili pepper, without seeds, chopped thinly

salt and black pepper

2 tbsp red pesto

1 tbsp pine nuts

Method

Cut the meat into ½ in/1cm wide strips from the long side of the fillet.

Lay the strips in a glass or earthenware dish. Put all the marinade ingredients in a bowl, mix well and then pour marinade over the strips of chicken. Let the chicken stand for about 30 minutes to marinate.

Beat the egg whites stiffly and carefully add the flour and lemon juice to make the batter. Take the chicken out of the marinade and set the marinade aside.

Heat the oil to 350°F/180°C in a deep-fry pan. Pass the chicken strips through the batter and deep-fry for about 5 minutes until golden brown. Drain on paper towel. Repeat for the rest of the chicken.

Pour the marinade into a pan, add the chicken stock and bring to a boil.

Mix the lemon juice and flour together to form a smooth paste and add this to the stock mixture.

Stir until the sauce thickens. Serve the chicken fingers with the dip sauce as a snack or as a starter (garnished with salad).

Ingredients

2¼ lb/1kg chicken breast fillets

oil for deep-frying

For the marinade

2 tbsp soy sauce; ¼ cup sherry

1 tsp fresh ginger, grated

1 tsp lemon rind; 1 tsp sugar

For the batter

2 egg whites; ¼ cup flour

¼ cup lemon juice

For the dipping sauce

small portion of the marinade

½ cup chicken stock

2 tbsp cornstarch

2 tbsp lemon juice

Chicken Fingers

Method

Preheat oven to 400°F/200°C. Heat the butter and oil in a large frying pan and fry the garlic and onion. Chop the mushrooms finely in a food processor and add to the garlic-onion mixture. Fry gently for about another 5 minutes. Sprinkle the flour and mix well. Add the water or stock and stir until the sauce thickens and begins to bubble. Allow to cool, then add the chives and basil.

Lay a sheet of puff pastry on a flat surface. Spread one-sixth of the mushroom mixture over it and then sprinkle with a sixth of the finely chopped pistachio nuts. Roll the ends of the sheet towards one another and then fold in half to give the appearance of a thick tree trunk. Lay on its side and press firmly.

Cut into 8 pieces and place on a greased baking sheet. Repeat for the rest of the pastry. Place the rolls in the freezer for 5 minutes and then bake for 12 to 15 minutes in the oven until golden brown. Mix the herbs with the mayonnaise and leave to stand for at least 30 minutes.

Season with salt and pepper and serve with the pasties.

Tip

As these pasties can be frozen (baked or unbaked), you can prepare them days or weeks in advance.

Wild Mushroom Pasties

Ingredients

1 tbsp butter; 1 tbsp olive oil

2 cloves garlic, finely chopped

1 onion, finely chopped

7 oz/200g wild mushrooms

(porcini, shitake, chanterelle)

1 tbsp flour; 2 tbsp water/stock

2 tbsp finely cut chives

2 tbsp finely chopped basil

6 sheets puff pastry

2 tbsp roasted pistachio nuts, finely chopped

2 tbsp fresh coriander, finely chopped

2 tbsp fresh chives, finely chopped

1 tbsp fresh parsley, finely chopped

3/4 cup mayonnaise; salt and pepper

Method

Scrub the mussels well and remove beard. Dispose of any open or damaged mussels. Bring the wine, onion, parsley stalks, and black peppercorns to a boil in a large pan. Add the mussels (in two batches) and cover the pan. Cook for 3 to 4 minutes over high heat until they open. Shake the pan regularly. Throw the still-closed mussels or those with a strong odor away. Pour the stock in a measuring jug and allow to cool. Season with salt and pepper according to taste.

Prepare the crêpe batter. Put the flour in a bowl and add the eggs, stock, and 2 tablespoons of cream. Beat well, then leave the batter for 1 hour.

Melt 1 tablespoon of butter in a pan. Add the melted butter to the batter and beat. Heat another tablespoon of butter in the pan and distribute well. Pour some batter in the pan ($^3/_4$ cup per pancake).

Remove pan from the heat. Allow the batter to slide quickly to the center of the pan and then make circular movements so that the batter covers the entire bottom (remove excess as crêpes should be thin). Turn the heat up and shake the pan now and again, so that the crêpe does not stick. Fry both sides until they are golden brown. Slide the crêpe onto a plate, roll and keep warm while you prepare the other crêpes.

Heat the rest of the cream in a small pan and remove the mussels from their shell. Add the mussels to the cream and stir gently. Spoon some of the mussel mixture onto the edge of each pancake, sprinkle with parsley and then roll.

Serve immediately.

Crêpes Filled with Mussels

Ingredients

4$^1/_2$ lbs/2kg mussels

$^1/_2$ cup dry white wine

2 tbsp chopped onions

4 stalks of parsley, broken

6 black peppercorns, crushed

For the crêpes

$^3/_4$ cup flour

stock from the mussels (see step 2)

4-6 tbsp heavy cream; 4 tbsp butter

6 tbsp fresh parsley, finely chopped

2 large eggs

Method

Put the lemon juice, crushed garlic, and olive oil in a bowl and marinate the squid in this for at least 3 hours (preferably overnight).

Put all the ingredients for the dressing in another bowl and combine until the mixture thickens.

Heat 1 tablespoon of oil in the pan, add the marinated squid and cook for a few minutes until done.

You can also broil the calamari.

Sprinkle the calamari with the dressing and serve immediately.

Ingredients

2¼ lbs/2kg calamari, in thin rings

½ cup lemon juice

3 cloves garlic, crushed

½ cup olive oil

For the dressing

¼ cup lemon juice

½ cup olive oil

1½ tbsp fresh parsley, finely chopped

1 clove garlic, finely chopped

½ tsp Dijon mustard

salt and pepper

Marinated Calamari

Method

Put all the ingredients for the marinade in a large plastic bowl and mix. Add the pieces of lamb and cover well in marinade mixture. Cover the bowl and allow the meat to marinate in the fridge for about 1 hour. Soak them for 10 minutes in water if you are using wooden skewers.

Stir the apricots and mint into the lamb mixture and season with salt and pepper.

Take the pieces of meat and apricots out of the marinade and thread them onto 8 metal or wooden kebab skewers. Add lemon to the ends of each skewer. Dispose of the marinade.

Set the broiler to the highest temperature. Broil the kebabs for 8 to 10 minutes.

Turn them regularly until the meat turns brown. Pour the lemon juice over the kebabs and serve immediately.

Seasoned Lamb and Apricot Kebabs

Ingredients	For the marinade
1lb 2oz/500g lamb (leg), cubed	1 clove garlic, crushed
4oz/125g dried apricots	2 tbsp low fat yogurt
$\frac{1}{2}$ tsp fresh mint, finely chopped	1 tbsp olive oil; $\frac{1}{2}$ tsp cumin powder
salt and black pepper	$\frac{1}{2}$ tsp ground coriander; $\frac{1}{2}$ tsp paprika
1 lemon, in 8 segments	pinch of cayenne pepper; juice of 1 lemon

Method

Cut the chicken fillet into chunks of 1in/5cm.

Mix water, peanut butter, honey, soy sauce, lemon juice, sambal, ginger, and onion in a bowl. Add the chunks of chicken and allow to marinate for at least 2 hours.

Take the chicken chunks out of the marinade and set aside.

Pour the marinade into a pan, bring to a boil, set the heat to low and allow the marinade to reduce.

Thread two chicken chunks on each skewer, broil for 5 minutes and serve with the marinade.

Chicken Satay

Ingredients

1lb 2oz/500g chicken breast fillet

½ cup water

2 tbsp peanut butter

1 tbsp honey

1 tbsp mild soy sauce

2 tbsp lemon juice

½ tsp sambal oelek

½ tsp fresh ginger, grated

1 onion, finely chopped

wooden kebab skewers, soaked in water for 1 hour

Method

Halve the bell peppers and scoop out the seeds. Broil the peppers on a baking sheet at high temperature until they become blistered and begin to blacken.

Place in a plastic bag and allow to cool. Remove the skin and cut into thin strips.

Combine the strips of pepper with the scallions and mushrooms in a bowl.

Stir a mixture of garlic, mustard, Italian dressing, and herbs in a bowl and pour this sauce over the mushrooms. Stir gently, covering the peppers and mushrooms well with the mixture.

Cover the bowl and allow the peppers and mushrooms to marinate for about 4 hours.

Ingredients

1 red bell pepper

1 green bell pepper

1 yellow bell pepper

4 scallions, sliced

1 lb 2oz/500g mushrooms, halved

2 cloves garlic, crushed

1 tbsp coarse honey mustard

½ cup Italian salad dressing

2 tbsp fresh parsley, finely chopped

1 tbsp fresh thyme, finely chopped

Marinated Mushrooms

Method

Mix the olives, tarragon, chives, mint, and lemon rind in a bowl and add the ricotta. Season with salt and pepper and mix again. Add tomato puree, mix well, and spoon onto a serving dish.

Set the broiler to the highest temperature. Broil the slices of baguette for about 2 minutes until they are brown on both sides. Rub the garlic onto the bread well and serve with the dip.

Garlic Bread with Herb Dip

Ingredients

6 green olives, pitted, and finely chopped

1 tbsp tarragon; 1 tbsp chives; 1 tbsp mint

1 tsp grated lemon rind

9 oz/250g ricotta cheese; black pepper

4 tbsp sun-dried tomato puree

1 baguette, in ½ in/2cm thick slices

1 clove garlic, halved

tapas

Method

Cut off the mushroom stalks.

Clean the caps well with a damp cloth.

Brush the inside of the caps with the vinaigrette.

Prepare a stuffing of crab meat, mayonnaise, scallion, parsley, and walnuts in a bowl.

Mix well and season with salt and pepper.

Stuff the caps with a heaping teaspoon of the crab stuffing.

Keep the stuffed mushrooms in the fridge.

Ingredients

50 mushrooms

vinaigrette

2 cans (6oz/170g each) crab meat

2 tbsp mayonnaise

2 tbsp scallion, finely chopped

2 tbsp fresh parsley, finely chopped

4 oz/100g walnuts, finely chopped

salt and freshly ground black pepper

Crab and Walnut Stuffed Mushrooms

Method

Heat the oil in a nonstick frying pan (diameter 9 in/22cm) and add the finely

chopped onions evenly over the pan. Place the thin slices of potato on the onions.

Cover the pan with tin foil and fry the potato for about 30 minutes over low heat

until soft.

Arrange the asparagus, strips of chili pepper, and zucchini (like spokes of

a wheel) on top of the layer of potatoes. Pour over the beaten eggs and sprinkle

with pepper and Parmesan cheese.

Place the frittata under a preheated broiler for about 15 minutes until firm.

Allow the frittato to cool for about 10 minutes before removing it from the pan.

Cut in wedges and serve immediately.

Vegetable Frittata

Ingredients

2 tbsp vegetable oil

1 onion, finely chopped

1 potato, in very thin slices

12oz/350g can asparagus, drained

1 red chili pepper, in long strips

1 zucchini, in long strips

6 eggs, beaten

freshly ground black pepper

2 tbsp Parmesan cheese, grated

Method

Prepare a dressing of olive oil, lemon juice, and capers in a bowl.

Arrange the smoked salmon and onion on four plates.

Sprinkle the salmon with the dressing and scatter with parsley and black pepper.

Garnish the carpaccio with the extra capers and serve immediately.

Ingredients

¼ cup olive oil, extra virgin

⅛ cup lemon juice

1 tsp capers

12 oz/350g smoked salmon, 3-4 slices per person

1 small red onion, finely chopped

1 tbsp fresh parsley, roughly chopped

freshly ground black pepper

capers for garnishing

Smoked Salmon Carpaccio

Method

Cut the olives lengthwise with a sharp knife and remove pits. Add the olives to the oregano, thyme, rosemary, bay leaves, fennel seeds, cumin, chili pepper, and garlic and mix well in a bowl.

Scoop the olive mixture into a sealable pot. Pour oil into it until covered and close the pot for at least three days. Shake the pot before use.

Seasoned Olives

Ingredients

1lb 2oz/500g black olives

1 sprig oregano

1 sprig thyme

½ tsp fresh rosemary, finely chopped

½ tsp fennel seeds, crushed

½ tsp cumin seeds, finely crushed

½ red chili pepper, without seeds, finely chopped

4 cloves garlic, crushed

2 bay leaves

olive oil

Method

Heat the oil over moderate heat in a wok.

Add the garlic and the chili peppers, then stir-fry for about 1 minute.

Add the shrimp and stir-fry for another 2 minutes until the shrimp has changed color.

Add the tomato juice and the soy sauce, while stirring the brown sugar, then stir-fry for another 3 minutes.

Serve the stir-fry dish hot.

Ingredients

½ tsp vegetable oil

½ tsp sesame seed oil

3 cloves garlic, crushed

3 red chili peppers, finely chopped

2¼ lb/1kg shrimp, peeled

1 tbsp brown sugar

½ cup tomato juice

1 tbsp soy sauce

Shrimp with Chili Peppers

Method

Pour the lemon juice into a small pan and add sugar. Heat the mixture over low heat and dissolve the sugar. Cook the mixture until it thickens. Pour into a jug and allow to cool for 20 minutes. Place the syrup for at least 1 hour (preferably overnight) in the fridge.

Cut off the melon skin and remove the seeds. Cut the fruit flesh into pieces and pour the released melon juice into a bowl. Scatter finely chopped mint over the melon and mix carefully. Add the melon juice to the cold syrup.

Pour the syrup over the pieces of melon shortly before serving. Sprinkle the melon with grated lemon rind.

Watermelon with Lemon Syrup

Ingredients

juice of 1 lemon

2 tbsp fine crystal sugar

2¼lbs/1kg watermelon

1 tbsp mint, finely chopped

grated lemon rind

Method

Mix the smelt in the food processor.

Put the fish puree in a bowl and add the shallots, dill, lemon rind and juice, flour, and eggs. Season with salt and pepper.
Mix well.

Heat the oil in a pan and add the fish puree (1 tablespoon per fritter) and fry for 2 to 3 minutes until golden brown. Serve with lemon segments.

Ingredients

1lb 2 oz/500g smelt

4 tbsp shallots, finely chopped

2 tbsp fresh dill, finely chopped

rind of 2 lemons

1 tsp lemon juice

$\frac{1}{2}$ cup flour

2 eggs, lightly beaten

freshly ground pepper and salt

olive oil for frying

Fish Frittatas

Index